How The F✓k Are You Still President

Written and illustrated by
John Spreincer McKellyanne Huckamucci

ISBN: 978-0-9885273-5-5

First edition November 2019.

By reading, understanding and not immediately violating this legalese, you
are by default a better lawyer than Rudy Giuliani. Congratulations to you.
Let your family know.

Dedicated to everyone in Wisconsin, Michigan, Florida and Pennsylvania who voted for Jill Stein in 2016.

"Who, me?" Yeah, you. I bet you don't talk about that so much these days, do you? You thought Hillary was going to skate to an easy win, so you stood in line for three hours and voted for a lousy candidate with no chance just so you could tell people you did so, because you thought voting for a third party candidate would give you an air of mystery or at least some social media likes. But then that didn't happen, and on top of everything else that's gone wrong, you're as uninteresting at parties as ever. Oh, you don't like the beer I'm drinking anymore since the brewery that distributes it started selling it at grocery stores? Shut up.

Dedicated similarly to every 2020 voter who intends to vote for Tulsi Gabbard over the Democratic candidate if she runs as an independent. May a portal to Antarctica open beneath the voting booth as soon as you step inside.

Rise and shine, Mr. President!
You've got an important job to do!

Oh right, fuck me, nevermind, just kidding.

Because somehow the president is still you.

Now where the fuck did you go this time?

To your Florida office on the back nine?

Another vacation on America's dime?

Another stupid rally where
you pretend you're the divine?

To some beloved tyrant's castle
for a pep talk and wine?

You know what, forget it.
I don't care, it's fine.

It's not like you'd do your fucking job if you were home.

You'd just sulk around like a teen,
face glued to your phone.

Tweeting here, tweeting there,
shitposts fouling up the joint.

I'd tell you to stop tweeting,
but what's the fucking point?

NEW PHONES

BATTERY
DIED —
THROW
AWAY!!

es." Will someone from his desk at all
d starved regime please inform him that I
have a Nuclear Button, but it is a much
er & more powerful one than his, and my
on works!

- Jan 2, 2018

@rEaLD...

Democrats just blocked @Fox...m
holding a debate. Good, then I think I'll do the
same thing with the Fake News Networks and
the Radical Left Democrats in the General
Election debates!

6:05 PM - Mar 6, 2019

Donald J Trump
@rEaLDoNaLdTrUmP

addition to winning the Electoral College in a
ndslide, I won the popular vote if you deduct
e millions of people who voted illegally

Donald J Trump
@rEaLDoNaLdTrUmP

PY NEW YEAR TO EVERYONE,
LUDING THE HATERS AND THE FAKE
VS MEDIA! 2019 WILL BE A FANTASTIC
R FOR THOSE NOT SUFFERING FROM
MP DERANGEMENT SYNDROME. JUST
M DOWN AND ENJOY THE RIDE, GREAT

ailing New York Times that the corrupt former
loaders of the FBI, almost all fired or forced to leave the agency for some
very bad reasons, opened up an investigation on me, for no reason & with
no proof, after I fired Lyin' James Comey, a total sleaze!

6:05 AM - Jan 12, 2019

Donald J Trump
@rEaLDoNaLdTrUmP

.Funny thing about James Comey. Everybody wanted him fired, Republican
d Democrat alike. After the rigged & botched Crooked Hillary
vestigation, where she was interviewed on July 4th Weekend, not recorded
sworn in, and where she said she didn't know anything (a lie),....

AM - Jan 12, 2019

Donald J Trump
@rEaLDoNaLdTrUmP

FBI was in complete turmoil (see N.Y.
hip and the way he handle
on of powers from the Jus
Comey was a great day for Americ

6:53 AM - Jan 12, 2019

Donald J Trump
@rEaLDoNaLdTrUmP

.....who is being totally protected by h
Angry Democrats – leaking machines
the Real Collusion (and much more) by
Campaign, and the Democratic Nationa

7:09 AM - Jan 12, 2019

Donald J Trump
@rEaLDoNaLdTrUmP

have been FAR tougher on Russia than Oba
tougher than any other President. At the sar
getting along with Russia is a good thing, no
someone we will have good relations with Ru

20 AM - Jan 12, 2019

Donald J Trump
@rEaLDoNaLdTrUmP

....The Fake News is not as important, or
Social Media. They have lost tremendous
day in November, 2016, that I came down
with the person who was to become your
When I ultimately leave office in six......

6:30 AM - Jul 11, 2019

Donald J Trump
@rEaLDoNaLdTrUmP

...or a very nervous and skinny version o
(1000/24th), as your President, rather th
so great looking and smart, a true Stable
that even Social Media would be driven

Well it's fine, go and hide.
We'll put someone on TV to explain.
OH FUCK HE SAID WHAT?
OH FUCK GODDAMMIT NOT AGAIN.

Come Lindsey! Come Mitch!
Come Rand and Matt Gaetz!
On Kellyanne, Jared and Ivanka!
And those creepy sons you hate!

TRUMP ATTORNEY RUDY GIULIANI REACTS TO STATEMENT FROM RUDY GIULIANI

FOX NEWS ALERT

FOX NEWS LIVE

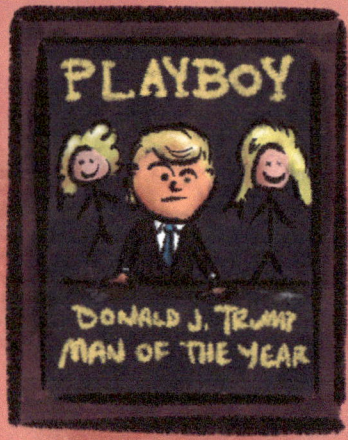

All this just to win another election?
You didn't even want to win the first time!

But then you did, and haven't shut up about it since.
Gloating "306" and "2016" while your other numbers decline.

You've been chasing that high ever since.
Like all of this was by design.

But the truth is you'll never be free again.
Lawsuits and charges until the end of time.

SUBPO
LAWSUITS

How the fuck are you still president, I asked,
but the answer is loud and crystal clear.
Without this job, you're no longer above the law,
and then all that loyalty will disappear.

So go off and hide, you traitorous little phony.
But the walls are closing in, and your future's looking lonely.

And before you run away, one last thing to remember:

If the law doesn't come for you soon,
we'll be ready come November.

About the Author

John Spreincer McKellyanne Huckamucci hopes to be done writing about this idiot. Vote Blue in 2020.

Also available in case you need more

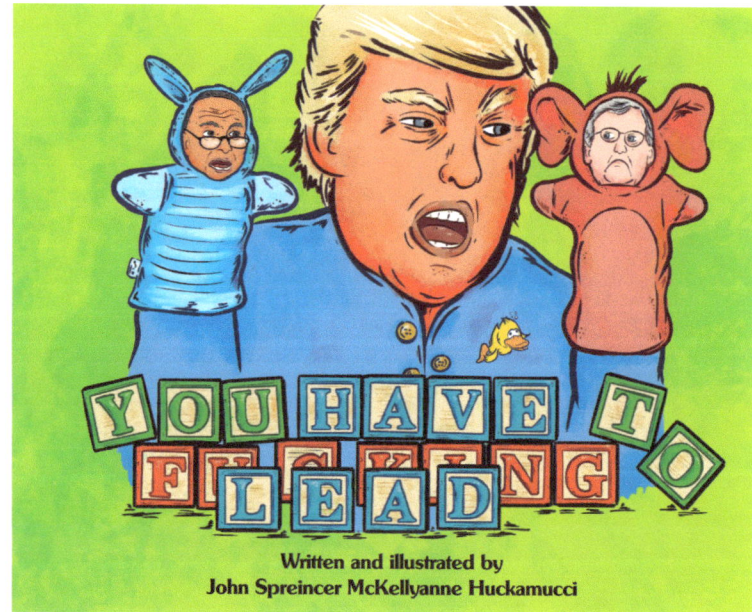

impeachvent.com